What Parents are saying about

Boys Alive! Bring Out Their Best! Workshops

"I feel more empowered as a parent and hope I will be more in tune with my boy. I have a greater understanding of where he is coming from."

"[Your workshop] was extremely insightful and I have a lot to contemplate and utilize."

"You have keen insight and share that in a most pleasant way."

"[I have a new] willingness to be more present with how my boys are. [I'll] remember to join in on the fun and to nurture the creativeness in [their] play."

"[I've experienced] a shift in perspective to viewing my boy's hard-wired energy level as a positive, rather than seeing the down-side of it. I hope to find more ways to provide the adventure he needs day-to-day, not just in special outings and events."

"The differences between male and female are indeed genetic and pre-determined. [I've learned how] to change my 'negative' interactions with my child – turn it around, reinterpret, change my reaction."

"I have learned to be more direct in getting positive behavior."

"[Now I know] that my boys are acting as they do because of who they are, and that it's counterproductive and pointless to want them to be something else."

"I want my wife to come the next time…not for our son…but so that she can understand me!"

"The information you've given me today will help greatly with my most challenging and wonderful 7-year old boy!"

"[I realize] that boys are <u>boys</u> and to not forget that simple but powerful force."

"[I have] to get 'out of the way' of my 3 boys. I have a new, deep understanding of [them]. I <u>get</u> that they <u>need</u> to make jabs in the air, swing bats, punch each other a little, <u>barge</u> into rooms, slam doors and <u>drop</u> toilet seats. I need to get over this when it's not hurting anybody. Also need to take a few precious breakable things and put them away, even though they are not little kids."

"I do deeply appreciate your offering. It is very difficult to step out of subtly undermining who my boy is in his natural ways and timing. The workshop was a very important frame-shift for me."

"[Now I know that] my 2-year old boy's wiring and natural growth cycle will not be congruent with the 'clean house, perfect looking home' and will be more fulfilling with more moving, jobs and action, etc."

"Sometimes I feel like my boy has a problem because he hits, or that somehow I am failing because he hits. Today I learned to accept <u>all</u> of him and use his hitting as a cue to offer a new environment (outside) or more physical activity."

"The concept of less visual stimulus in our home environment is something new and I would love to try to implement it. We have far too much 'stuff' littering our lives. Thank you for that."

"Can I take you home with me?"

Contact Janet Allison for information about offering a Boys Alive! workshop in your school or community.

Boys Alive!
Bring Out Their Best!

Why 'boys will be boys' and how you
can guide them to be their best
at home and at school.

Janet Allison

www.parenting-advice-from-mom.com

parenting-advice-from-mom.com
2010

For Mom and Dad,
Katie and Anna.

And with gratitude to all of my teachers,
in person and in print.

DISCLAIMER

This book details the author's personal experiences with and opinions about teaching and parenting boys. The author is not a healthcare provider.

The author and publisher are providing this book and its contents on an "as is" basis and make no representations or warranties of any kind with respect to this book or its contents. The author and publisher disclaim all such representations and warranties, including for example warranties of merchantability and healthcare for a particular purpose. In addition, the author and publisher do not represent or warrant that the information accessible via this book is accurate, complete or current.

The statements made about products and services have not been evaluated by the U.S. Food and Drug Administration. They are not intended to diagnose, treat, cure, or prevent any condition or disease. Please consult with your own physician or healthcare specialist regarding the suggestions and recommendations made in this book.

Except as specifically stated in this book, neither the author or publisher, nor any authors, contributors, or other representatives will be liable for damages arising out of or in connection with the use of this book. This is a comprehensive limitation of liability that applies to all damages of any kind, including (without limitation) compensatory; direct, indirect or consequential damages; loss of data, income or profit; loss of or damage to property and claims of third parties.

You understand that this book is not intended as a substitute for consultation with a licensed healthcare practitioner, such as your physician. Before you begin any healthcare program, or change your lifestyle in any way, you will consult your physician or other *licensed healthcare practitioner to ensure that you are in good health and that the examples contained in this book will not harm you.*

This book provides content related to topics physical and/or mental health issues. As such, use of this book implies your acceptance of this disclaimer.

Table of Contents

About Boys Alive! Bring Out Their Best!

It has been said that, "Parenting is the *hardest job you'll ever love*."

<u>Loving</u> our children is easy.

<u>Parenting them</u> is far more complex and exhausting!

Our children grow and learn every day, changing at lightning speed.

Are you changing enough to keep up with them?

Boys Alive! guides you to making positive, long-lasting change; for yourself, your boy and your family. It combines the wisdom of scientific and educational research with practical parenting skills, showing you new ways to bring out your boy's best at home and at school.

With your new skills,
you can guide him to become a man you are proud of.

Boys Alive! gathers wisdom from diverse fields of study:

- **Waldorf Education** – Preschool teacher Sharifa Oppenheimer and class teacher Jack Petrash, along with the author's own teaching experiences, combine to show you what children need at each age and stage of development.

- **Neuro-Linguistic Programming** – Understanding some fundamentals of verbal and non-verbal communication, along with observing your boy in unique ways, will help you understand the dynamics that exist in your relationship.

- **Brain research** – With new technologies that allow researchers like Dr. Daniel Amen and Dr. John Medina to look into the active brain, structural differences between the male and female brain continue to be revealed, making more sense of what we already know intuitively.

- **Gender Intelligence** – Boys and girls need different approaches to learning and Michael Gurian and Dr. Leonard Sax have done extensive research on the effective teaching strategies that each gender needs.

Parenting is a grand experiment!

I encourage you to put these ideas into practice, changing and modifying as you go…just as your boy does every day. My hope is that you will return to Boys Alive! often, discovering a new nugget of wisdom at just the time you need it!

Boys Alive! is a valuable resource for teachers, too!

About the Author

Janet Allison is the mom of two wonderfully grown daughters and has been a teacher to many children. Her first Waldorf class began with 10 boys and 2 girls. The boys were energetic, restless and surprising. She quickly learned that boys approach their learning differently and need to be taught and parented in new ways.

In the years since then, her studies of child development, brain science, and gender intelligence have confirmed what she knew intuitively. One of Ms. Allison's gifts lies in translating vast research into the practical skills that enable parents and teachers to accept and guide the enthusiasm, energy and creativity that boys bring to school and home.

She graduated with a B.S. in Elementary Education, *cum laude*, from the University of Maine at Farmington. She has studied Waldorf Education extensively and has a Master's certificate in Neuro-Linguistic Programming (NLP). Her teachers include Lindagail Campbell, Michael Grinder, and those at the Gurian Institute.

Janet Allison teaches *Boys Alive! Bring Out their Best!* workshops for parents and teachers. She teaches extensively in the Pacific Northwest and will travel to your community or school. In addition to being a Parent Educator, she is an Educational Consultant, specializing in

Waldorf Education and a Family Coach. Her previous book is *Discover What You Believe About Being a Parent,* available at her website.

She is currently at work on *Girls Alive! Bring Out Their Best!*

Portland, Oregon
February 2010

1. What Changes Do You Want to Make?

CHANGE is the first step... but *what* should change?!

"When you change the way you look at things,
the things you look at change."

~ *John Grinder, co-founder of NLP*

Just by opening *Boys Alive!* you have set the wheels of change in motion. You may soon find some of your ideas and thoughts beginning to change. When they do, your words and your responses to others begin to change, too.

This is the beginning of a *cascading effect* that may be so subtle at first that you hardly notice. Soon, though, you'll realize that you've begun to make some positive changes and, as a result, your boy happens to be changing, too!

Often, when we say '*I want things to change*', we forget to clearly specify what we want those changes to be.

Begin considering the changes you want to make by asking yourself...

- *How do I want things to become for myself?*

- *How do I want things to become for my boy?*

- *How do I want things to become in my family?*

It is important for you to be *very specific* about the changes you want to make.

When you are able to say…

- What you will **hear**: *"I'll hear the sound of laughter as I enjoy making dinner with my son."*

- What you will **see**: *"I'll see my two boys playing together in their sand box."*

- What you will **feel**: *"My breath will be steady and calm as we leave for school in the morning."*

…then, and only then, can your unconscious mind begin the rehearsal it needs in order to make those changes a reality.

Just as elite athletes practice the perfect game in their minds, your mind will begin to organize *your thoughts, your words, and your actions* and your 'ball-of-change' is rolling!

When you know what you want to *change to*, you may even find that you are surprised by new opportunities that you hadn't even considered before!

Watch for new possibilities!

3 Rules for Change

- *Change must be stated in the positive.* This is when you get to say what you DO want, not what you *don't* want.

- *Change must begin with and be controlled by you.* Only <u>you</u> can instigate change.

- *Change must be a do-able size.* We all want to end world hunger, yet we have to begin with a do-able task.

- *Change affects others.* Consider how your changes will impact others around you.

Choosing your Changes

Do you want to change how you are parenting?

When you add more knowledge upon which to base your approach and responses, you'll be parenting with more wisdom and more choices.

Do you want to enable your boy to be the best he can be?

When you know how his brain works and what he needs to be able to learn, you'll be able to make changes in your home and school environment to support him.

Do you want to change your family's dynamics?

You and your parenting partner can make conscious choices about how you want your family to be. Often, we fall back into the old habits and family patterns that we were raised with.

While some of those traditions and habits can work in your family now, there may be some that no longer serve you and your family in beneficial ways.

Acknowledging those that are still useful and letting go of those that no longer work means that you are creating your own healthy and up-to-date family culture.

A note of caution about Change

Change can be messy. Change may feel like chaos at first. As change continues, order resumes, and you feel comfortable again…until the next change! Stay with it! Some say that change takes 21 days to become a habit, so stay with it long enough for the change to manifest.

How will your Change affect others?

It is important to consider the changes you want to make and how they fit within the larger context of all of your relationships.

Ask yourself...

- *"What will improve?"*
- *"What will be at risk?"*

Does the change match what you believe and value in your life? Does the change align with all the areas of your life - as a person, as a parent, and as a partner?

When you make changes that do <u>not</u> align with your beliefs and values, you are setting yourself up for frustration and failure.

Perhaps you aren't sure what you believe and value about being a parent?

When you were pregnant you may have spent time thinking about this but when the diapers are dirty and the dishes are dirty and you are exhausted, you are more interested in coping with the here and now and may have forgotten about this important cornerstone of your parenting.

How are your beliefs and values aligned with your parenting partner? Do you share the same beliefs and values? For example, if you believe that a messy house means your children are creative and your partner believes that a messy house means your children are disobedient...well, then, you've got conflict!

A separate workbook, *Discover What You Believe about Being a Parent,* guides you step-by-step to these all-important discoveries. Find it at: www.parenting-advice-from-mom.com

As you begin

Because your changes have already begun – just by opening *Boys Alive!* – it is important to take note of this moment. Writing a letter to yourself is one way to mark this moment. Writing to yourself may be easier if you imagine that you are your best friend, offering yourself encouragement and acknowledging the hard work that may be ahead of you.

Be sure to tell yourself that you believe in yourself, that you are capable of making changes and you are in control of creating the life and family that you want.

After all, this is your life and it is not a dress rehearsal!

Letter to myself ...

Date: _____

What Changes do you want to make?

Now begin to *write your new life!* When you get specific about the changes you want to make, you are creating your life the way you want it to be.

You've heard the quote...*Be careful what you wish for!*...Be careful to make your desires specific and do-able.

1. One thing I would like to change about my parenting style is:

2. One thing I would like to change between my children is:

3. One thing I would like to change with my partner is:

4. One thing I would like to change about our household routine is:

5. One thing I would like to change about my boy's habits is:

6. One thing I would like to change about my boy's helpfulness is:

7. One thing I would like to change about my boy's social life is:

8. One thing I would like to change about my boy's school life is:

9. One thing I would like to change about my boy's friends is:

10. One thing I would like to change about myself is:

11. Add any other changes you'd like to make for yourself:

As you consider these questions, I encourage you to notice what is important to you. (You may already be well-attuned to what bothers you!)

Begin to acknowledge, out loud, what pleases you. Often, simply speaking what is positive and working amplifies that very thing.

When you have thoughtfully considered how your life is now, you'll be well on your way to making positive changes for yourself.

As you change, you'll notice change begins rippling out from you, like that of a pebble tossed into a still pond.

Prepare to be surprised!

> *You've got to <u>want</u> to change,*
> *<u>know how</u> to change,*
> *And give yourself*
> *the <u>chance</u> to change!*
> *~John Grinder*

Meanwhile…keep lovin' your boy!

2. Considering His Past

As you begin, take a moment to thank yourself for honestly considering the places in your life where you are ready to welcome change.   And thank yourself for acknowledging what is easy to love and more difficult to love about your boy.

Take a moment to do that now…

A note about the Dynamic Line Drawing above...
To clear your mind and set aside the busyness of family, work, play and friends, each chapter begins with a review and an opportunity to reflect on the insights and achievements you've made so far.

Trace the lines with your eyes and index finger, beginning and ending wherever feels right to you.

When you reach a place where the lines cross, pause and take a deep breath, allowing your mind to clear even more. As you trace the form, relax your jaw, your neck and your shoulders.

Making Changes means...

- Stating the change you want to make in the positive

- Knowing you are the only one that can change

- Making the change you want into a do-able size

- Assessing the impact of your change on others around you

And because you are reading this, it is likely you want to make changes that will improve your relationship with your boy, but first...

Who *is* your Boy?

This writing exercise will take time. I encourage you to revisit it often as you talk with your partner, parents, friends, and others on your parenting team who know and love your boy.

Keep adding to your vision of your boy. What do *you* remember? What do *they* remember?

> *"If you want to change something, observe it."*
>
> ~Gustav Heinemann

Consider his Past

1. Before you had children, what did you imagine about parenting? Did you daydream about what life was going to be like? What were your beliefs about being a parent?

2. How have those ideals changed?

3. How does the way you were parented influence how you are parenting now? How do you parent the same? How do you parent differently?

4. What did you imagine about your baby when you were pregnant? Did you know he was a boy? Did he have a pre-birth nickname? Does he fit that now? If you didn't know his gender, what were your thoughts upon learning that you had a boy?

5. What were your feelings the first time you gazed into your boy's eyes?

6. What were those first days like? How did he relate to you? Did he make eye contact? Smile? Coo? Did he have colicky cries? Did he sleep? Or was he often awake? What was your activity level? What was the activity level of your household?

7. Were there others helping to care for baby and you? What comments did they make about the baby? It may be helpful to go back to his baby book and relive those first days.

8. When you close your eyes and think about those early days, what pictures, sounds, smells or feelings come to mind?

Continue to reflect upon and add to these thoughts about who your boy has been <u>up until now</u>. These are observations only and can be completely free of judgement.

Making changes now may save you from regrets later…

> *If I had my child to raise all over again,*
> *I'd build self-esteem first, and the house later.*
> *I'd finger-paint more, and point the finger less.*
> *I would do less correcting and more connecting.*
> *I'd take my eyes off my watch, and watch with my eyes.*
> *I'd take more hikes and fly more kites.*
> *I'd stop playing serious, and seriously play.*
> *I would run through more fields and gaze at more stars.*
> *I'd do more hugging and less tugging.*
>
> *~Diane Loomans*
> *from "If I Had My Child to Raise Over Again"*

The past is behind you…

Change begins *now* and moves forward.

Meanwhile…keep lovin' your boy!

3. Considering His Present

As you begin, take a moment to thank yourself for taking the time to reflect on your boy's past without judging him, yourself or others.

Take a moment to do that now...

Observing your boy

You may feel like you look at your boy *all the time* but do you <u>really see him</u>? When we take time to *truly see* another person, or a flower, or a tree, we see elements we hadn't noticed before.

Give yourself time to observe your boy. Watch him when he plays, eats, sleeps. Look past his outer skin and imagine the muscles and bones that shape your boy, the energy and imagination that make him who he is.

You can't really know another person until you've walked a mile in his shoes.

Consider his Present

1. What kind of play does he engage in each day? Does he play by himself? Does he want you to play with him?

2. What is his general overall mood? Is he quiet, fidgety, active or pensive?

3. What are his favorites? Food, games, sports, books…ask him!

4. What are his dislikes? Ask him!

5. Practice being him – stand like he does, gesture like he does, eat like he does. What is unique about him? What family characteristics does he have?

6. Drawing your boy is a way to deeply observe him. Do some quick line drawings as he goes about his day. Try a more detailed sketch when he is sleeping. (Or sculpt him or paint him…) *No artistic experience necessary…these drawings are only for you.*

Sketches of my boy...

Date: _____

You may find that your understanding of and connection with your boy deepens as you *'walk in his shoes.'*

Enjoy experiencing your boy fully and completely *in the present.*

Meanwhile…keep lovin' your boy!

4. Considering His Future

As you begin, take a moment to thank yourself for observing your boy keenly and getting to know him more deeply as he is *right now*.

Take a moment to do that now…

Where do the Changes lead?

As with all change, it is imperative that you know what the change is *leading towards*.

The last step in developing a full picture of your boy is to consider his future. Imagine your boy at any age you choose…

- 18 and going off to college
- 30 and getting married
- 60 and enjoying grandchildren

Whatever age you choose, be sure to be specific and fully imagine that age and the experiences that come with each unique stage of life.

In *Simplicity Parenting* , Kim John Payne said, *"When you create a mental image of your hopes, you chart a course. You create a picture you can then step into...*

Consider his Future

1. Describe in great detail what you imagine his life might be like: Will he have a family? Pets? Will he live in a house or an apartment?

2. Who will his friends be? What will his passions be? What jobs will he have? What will his days be like?

3. How will he be in relation with you? How will he be in relation with his siblings?

4. Write and draw this scenario, fully and completely, and revisit it often to add more detail.

You are drawing his map,
plotting the course for his future.

Sure, he will grow up, no matter what. Yet, will you have given him the guidance he needs in the specific ways that he needs it? Will you have given forethought to how you want him to grow?

When you take time to imagine his future, it is *"like a lasso thrown around a star, your imagination navigates the surest path to your goal."* ~Kim John Payne

Review your notes and begin to list the qualities that show up in what you've written. It might look something like...

Courage	*Carelessness*
Laziness	*Enthusiasm*
Patience	*Empathy*

Be neutral and be honest.

_____   _____

_____   _____

_____   _____

Noting these qualities <u>now</u> shows you areas you may want to emphasize (or minimize) in your day-to-day parenting.

Begin charting his course now.

> *"The best time to plant a tree was 20 years ago."*
>
> ~Chinese proverb

Meanwhile... keep lovin' your boy!

5. How Do You See Yourself?

As you begin, take a moment to thank yourself for creating a lively, honest and judgment-free portrait of your boy: past, present and future.

Take a moment to do that now…

Connecting with Your Deeper Self

Up until now, you have been taking a deep look at your son. Now it is your turn! This is an opportunity to look deeply within yourself, as your journey to a new awareness in your parenting develops and strengthens.

Often, the only time we pause to take stock of our lives is at New Year's or perhaps on a significant birthday. And it often backfires! Who hasn't set unrealistic, soon-forgotten goals for themselves?

Just as with your boy, finding out where you are *now*, will help you decide where you want to go in the future.

As the poet Mary Oliver asks…

"Tell me, what will you do with your one wild and precious life?"

The Wheel of Your Life

Many cultures use circles as a way to represent the continuum of life and a connection to something greater. It is also a way of looking at your life, at this moment, right now, with *you* as the center of the universe. What will the Wheel of Your Life tell you?

Consider the following exercise a snapshot of your *"one wild and precious life."*

DATE: _____

With colored pencils, fill each area according to how full and satisfying it is for you, today, suspending judgment, just noticing how each area contributes its part to making up the wheel of your whole life.

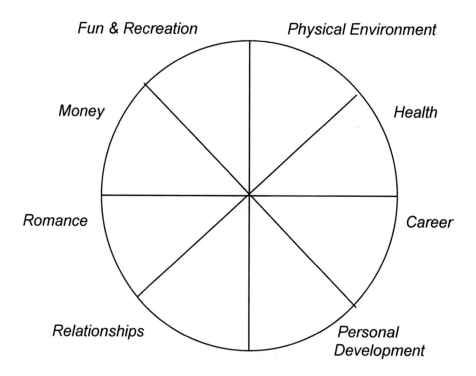

(Be sure to date this wheel… you may be surprised to see how the sections change between now and when you color another wheel at the end of this book).

Now, imagine that the Wheel of Your Life is a wheel on a bicycle. How is your ride? Is it feeling a little bumpy? Or perhaps it is really rocky!? How can you begin to make your ride smoother?

Changing Your Ride

Choose a section of the wheel that you would like to change...

1. Describe how that section is for you *now*. Be specific!

2. Imagine what changes would be needed to smooth out your ride. What can you add or take away? Be as specific as possible in your descriptions. You are creating your future!

3. What will you see, hear, and feel when your ride is just the way you want it to be?

You can continue this exercise on your own, completing each section.

Remember, where you give your attention is where change begins to happen!

> *If you can imagine it, you can achieve it.*
> *If you can dream it, you can become it.*
> *-William Arthur Ward*

Meanwhile... keep lovin' your boy!

6. A Mom's Letter to Her Son

As you begin, take a moment to thank yourself for looking deeply into your *'one wild and precious life'* and being willing to explore the changes that will make your life-ride even smoother.

Take a moment to do that now…

The Zen of Parenting

Have you experienced the *Zen of Parenting?* That's the rare moment when you realize that your parenting is going really well! You may just get a glimpse but when you are 'on your game' you are a much more creative, adaptive and energetic parent.

To be your best, your own self-care must be re-affirmed constantly because, as Sharifa Oppenheimer, author of *Heaven on Earth,* said, *"The most important gift we can give our children is a happy, well-rested parent; their well-being depends on us."*

A Gift for You

You've probably heard it a million times already...*"They grow up so fast...They'll be gone before you know it...Enjoy every moment."* And so you do...or you try to...but some days you simply succumb to the spilled milk and dirty socks! I invite you to take a moment away from the chaos, put your feet up, and enjoy this letter written by a mom to her son for his 21st birthday.

Happy Birthday to you!

You're 21. Hard to believe.

Of course, you were born 21 years ago at 4:43 a.m.

It was the coldest day of the year...Robin and Gary came to the hospital to see you...

You were quite cute, very small, 7 lbs, 20 oz., 21 1/2 inches long...and quiet, well, mostly...

We were very happy and had no idea how life would change now that you were around.

We lived in a tiny house so we were able to keep things pretty much together...

Dad stayed home for at least two weeks because he didn't want to leave us...

The first day he drove away, he was back in about 20 minutes ...with a puppy that didn't really last very long...but we got over it. Life was full enough just with you...

Soon you were one.....and then two......and then three......and then four......you loved to dress up.....play in the weather...get into mischief... and we had to watch you every minute.

It wasn't that you were naughty...you were just into things... all the time.

You loved to play ball...you loved to cook...you loved to eat...and you loved to play outside...

School was okay, but you weren't especially easy for your teachers...ever...

So we tried lots of things to keep you going...music...classes to make you smart...classes to simply keep you busy...

You did like movies...but we tried to limit them, keep them wholesome so your mind could grow uninfluenced by the media...

And we took lots of trips...to keep life fun and interesting...

Pretty soon you were very cool. So cool that you were almost untouchable...and we were trying very hard to keep up with you...

So we took a very big trip to try and pull ourselves back together.

Dad and I would wake up early every morning, and over coffee, we would strategize about how to get through another day with you...

We managed. We fed you a lot......we tried to keep life full of surprises...and you did fine, but you missed your friends...and so back we came.

You had more free time when you came home than you'd ever had before and you really enjoyed computers...cell phones...and being cool...

High school was a great experience...you learned to drive...you played sports...you did a little music...you took photography...and you mostly played...

At some point you discovered drinking...

You had lots of parties...

We were not quite sure what to do about you...

However, you turned out fine...more than that, you've exceeded our hopes and our dreams, and we love you very much.

Happy Birthday, Alex. Have fun drinking beer legally...we'll have fun tonight opening presents...and thinking about what a great person you've turned out to be...our little Alex...

Love, Mom

Meanwhile...keep lovin' your boy!

(Special thanks to Sherry, FE, for sharing her letter.)

7. Be the Movie Director of Your Life!

As you begin, take a moment to thank yourself for simply being you, as you are and as you are becoming. Perhaps you'd like to begin a new activity that nurtures you? Acknowledge the difficulty - and necessity - of finding that time for yourself and make a specific, do-able plan for how you will begin.

Take a moment to do that now…

How do you and your boy interact?

When communication is going smoothly with your boy, you may not give it a second thought.

However, when things go wrong, you are often left to wonder, *"What exactly just happened there?!"*

The following exercise will help you to understand the complex dynamic that exist between you and your boy. Often, when an interaction is less than successful, you want to do it differently the next time…but how?

Begin by choosing an interaction with your boy that…

- Repeats

- Gives you less than satisfactory results

- You would like to change

(Many parents choose familiar interactions such as: bedtime, getting out of the house for school, chores or teeth-brushing.)

As you try this exercise for the first time, choose an interaction that is fairly mild. As you become more familiar with how the exercise works, you'll be able to use it for situations that are more heated.

Parents have said that this exercise allows them to better understand the perspective of their child. Their new insights allow them to adjust their voice tone, responses and even how they stand during an interaction.

The added perspective of a curious and loving Observer also gives valuable information that may not have been considered before.

Now, you get to be the Movie Director of your life!

To begin...

1. Choose a time and place where you will be able to complete this exercise in quiet and without interruption. It will take 20-25 minutes.

2. Ask a partner to read the following script in a warm and loving way. If you would prefer to work alone, you can read the script into a tape and play it back, being sure to leave pauses at the appropriate places (...).

3. Choose an interaction with your boy that you would like to improve. Initially, choose an interaction that is fairly mild. Later, you can repeat this exercise with interactions that are more heated.

4. Stand comfortably, with your eyes closed, so that you can step into the imaginary three points of a triangle: Self, Your Boy, Observer.

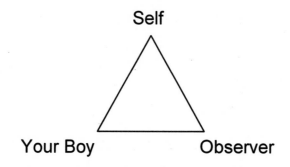

5. Your partner reads the following script slowly, pausing with the ellipses (…), and continuing when you've nodded your head to indicate you are ready.

Taking 3 deep breaths…and closing your eyes comfortably…settle yourself into your feet… your knees… your hips…and feeling your own feelings… hearing out of your own ears… seeing out of your own eyes…prepare to rerun a movie of your chosen situation from your own experience…

Begin the movie just before the situation became difficult or awkward…and run the movie from your own point of view… seeing what you saw… hearing what you heard… feeling what you felt…

Just view the movie… without judgment or criticism… just noticing the interaction…

[Pause here while the movie 'runs', wait for a nod]

And when you are ready… take a deep breath and move into the position of your boy…

And settle yourself into feeling like your boy… How is his posture?…What are his gestures?…Move your body…your

46

arms…your legs… so that you can get the feeling of how it is to be your boy in this interaction…

See out of your boy's own eyes… hear out of your boy's own ears…feel what your boy is feeling…and look out of his eyes to over to see that 'you over there'…

As you begin to run the movie again…

Notice what that 'you over there' is doing…how that 'you over there' is sounding… just notice… free of judgment… take in any new learning you might have from this position of being your boy…and seeing that 'you over there'…

[Pause here while the movie 'runs', wait for a nod]

And when you are ready… take a deep breath … as you step into the position of the observer…

This is a place of interested, loving curiosity…as you observe that 'you over there' and 'your boy over there' interacting with each other…

Go ahead and run the movie again… This time taking careful notice of the interplay between that 'you over there' and 'your boy over there'…

Staying free of judgment...being open to new insights and observations... continue to observe the movie to its logical end...

[Pause here while the movie 'runs', wait for a nod]

And when you are ready... take a deep breath... and return to the position of yourself... feeling your own feelings... seeing through your own eyes... and hearing through your own ears...That's right....Good...

And take a moment to thank yourself for participating in this exercise...acknowledging any new information and insights...as you open your eyes...and return to this room.

Thank your script reader for participating with you.

Now, take some time to reflect on your experience in each position...

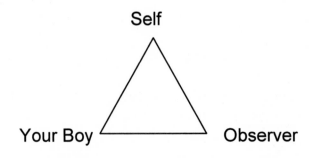

Self

Your Boy   Observer

1. How did each position feel? What did you notice?
Were you able to be equally at ease in each position?
(Many find one position to be more difficult than the
other two).

2. What new awareness did you have in the position of
'Your Boy'?

3. What new awareness did you have in the position of the curious, interested Observer?

4. What new information have you gained from your own point of view?

5. How can you apply that new information to the situation the next time?

6. Continue to be the Movie Director...and make *'The Sequel'*. Re-run your movie, including the new insights and information you've gained, and incorporate the changes that are now possible. (Remember, just like top athletes, you are creating your 'perfect parenting game'!)

When you practice *'stepping into someone else's shoes'* you gain more empathy, flexibility, and understanding of yourself and of the other person and that new awareness may begin to show up in *all* of your relationships.

---

*"Walk a mile in my shoes, walk a mile in my shoes.
Yeah, before you abuse, criticize and accuse,
walk a mile in my shoes."*

~Joe South and the Believers

Meanwhile...keep lovin' your boy!

8. Understanding Your Boy –
Why does he do that?!

As you begin, take a moment to thank yourself for reflecting on the different perspectives you are able to take when you want to deepen your understanding in any interaction. Standing strongly in your *Self*, stepping fully into the *Your Boy*, and being a curious and loving *Observer* means that you've expanded your ability to empathize and understand.

Take a moment to do that now…

Going *Back to the Future*

Take a step back in time…really, *really far* back in time…for here lies the true understanding of the differences between male and female and of *'why boys will be boys'*.

Imagine you are male... you travel each day over unfamiliar terrain (12 miles or more), crossing rivers, climbing hills and passing through forests and across grasslands. You are in search of animals to kill, to feed the women and children who await you back by the fire. You have your spear of sharpened rock, your fellow tribesmen, your wits and your good health.

What skills have you and your male tribe-mates developed over years and years of being **Hunters**?

_____   _____

_____   _____

_____   _____

Imagine you are female...you are sitting by a fire nursing your infant. You've spent the day harvesting seeds and grains and weaving their stalks into baskets while watching the young children play, chatting with your women tribe-mates and keeping an eye on the horizon for potential danger.

What skills have you and your female tribe-mates developed over years and years of being **Gatherers**?

_____   _____

_____   _____

_____   _____

As our ancestors learned to hunt, gather, and raise children, their brains developed the neural pathways necessary to the survival of our species. Male and female brains developed differently in order to accommodate the gender-specific tasks encountered in their environment.

We had to specialize to survive!

The Past Influences the Present

We have lived in Hunter-Gatherer-type societies for millions of years. We've been an agricultural society for about 10,000 years and an industrial society for only about the last 200 years. Our lives continue to have new challenges to which our brains must respond. Yet...

Our brains haven't evolved to meet the new demands!

Women were the Connectors

Their survival depended on their ability to relate to each other and to the hunters who provided food. Their children depended on them for care. Thus, the verbal and emotional centers of women's brains developed multiple areas to support a variety of interactions.

And the Gatherers

Women's work required attention to detail as they gathered seeds, roots and insects. This required finger dexterity and sensitivity and so their fine motor skills developed. Their slower-paced work allowed time for discussion. Women's bodies developed into a smaller, stronger stature, and they were able to endure greater hardships than men.

Men were the Providers

The Hunter's purpose was to provide food, protection, and plenty of sperm to fertilize the female's fewer eggs so the next generation could thrive. Planning, observing, and ingenuity were needed to support the tribe. An ability to see the landscape in his mind's eye allowed him to travel widely and always find his way home.

And the Hunters

With hunting came risk and self-sacrifice. It also required courage, aggressiveness, strong leadership, quick problem-solving and decisive action. Physically, hunting required short bursts of strong muscular activity and the muscle mass to fuel it. Single-focus on a target and hair-trigger responses ensured success. When the chase was on, there was no time to discuss, one person was in charge and the hunters did as they were told. During and after the hunt, there were long periods of rest, waiting for game to appear and resting up after an intense expenditure of energy.

What about now?

In the 21st century, the clear delineations of male and female roles have become ambiguous and murky, leaving many men confused.

- Jobs have changed from those requiring manual labor to those requiring communication and social skills.

- Women have become more confident, taking more control of their lives, leaving less room for men to be the providers.

- Typical male qualities, once highly valued, like: *exuberant energy, action and physical power* are now seen as liabilities because expectations of male behavior have shifted to: *'sit still and be quiet'* or *'tell me how you feel.'*

Adjusting expectations at home and school to allow for exuberant boy energy includes channeling it into meaningful work, providing outlets for his creative ingenuity, and giving him clear rules to follow.

<u>Every</u> behavior is useful in some context…

and it is crucial that we discover new contexts for boy energy!

What about Your Boy?

Imagine if your boy were raised on a farm in Kansas. He would be recognized and appreciated for his physical strength and vitality. His contributions to the family would be needed and valued.

Now imagine your same boy living in an apartment in the city. Imagine him in a traditional classroom. How will his energy and exuberance be perceived and received?

Reflections on your boy's environment

1. How does your boy's environment support his essential nature?

2. What elements of your boy's environment work against his essential nature?

3. What changes can be made in your home to support your boy?

4. What changes can be made in the other areas of his life to support his essential nature? (extra-curricular activities, school, clubs, etc.)

> *"You are not raising a little boy,*
> *You are raising a man."*
>
> ~ *P.Foner*

Meanwhile…keep lovin' your boy!

9. Looking Ahead

As you begin, take a moment to thank yourself for reflecting on the history of human development and considering how it has influenced the differences between male and female. Consider how boys and girls are affected now, as they strive to adapt to a society that has changed more quickly than the evolving brain could keep up with!

Take a moment to do that now...

Looking Ahead

The next seven sections explore communication basics along with your boy's biology, his hormones, and his development. With wisdom gleaned from the latest scientific findings and practical skills you can use immediately, you'll understand even more about the complexities that are at play in shaping your boy.

- **10. Communication Basics** – Knowing some basics of communication will increase your ability to connect with your boy.

- **11. Gender Differences** – His vision and hearing are only two of the structural differences between male and female. When you know what they are and how they differ, you can make adjustments to support his learning and behavior.

- **12. The Brain – His and Hers** - Not only will you understand your boy more clearly; you'll find this information insightful for your adult relationships, too!

- **13. Testosterone** – The hormone that 'drives the bus.' Understanding testosterone's role means you will know why your boy does flips with his skateboard and jumps off high places.

- **14. Ages and Stages** – When you understand where your boy is on the developmental continuum, you will know what he needs at each stage to help him be his best.

- **15. Peer Influence - Adult Influence** – Boys take more risks when in a group. Learn strategies to help him manage these impulses. Learn about the importance of Dad and other male role models for your boy.

- **16. At School** – Learn strategies you can share with his teachers so school can be a productive and boy-friendly place.

- **17. At Home** – Specific techniques for helping your boy take responsibility and participate fully in family life.

10. Communication Basics

As you begin, take a moment to thank yourself for getting this far! Your journey is about to get even more interesting as you learn communication skills, understand his brain and discover gender differences that perhaps you've sensed all along.

Take a moment to do that now...

Fundamentals

Understanding some fundamental principles of communication will support you in making effective changes in your current communication patterns with your boy. They may also change how you approach communication with others in your life, too!

John Grinder, co-founder of NLP (Neuro-Linguistic Programming), a study of language and communication once said... *"The meaning of your communication is the response that it gets."*

That means, if he isn't hearing you...it isn't his fault, necessarily. It means it is time for you to change <u>what</u> you are saying and <u>how</u> you are saying it.

These fundamental concepts will enable you to be more pro-active in all of your communication...

Non-Verbal Communication

Albert Mehrabian, in 1971, concluded that in any face-to-face communication there are three elements at play...

55% Body Language   38% Voice Tone   7% Words

Body Language and Eye Contact

- He reads what your body says before he even hears your words.
- He does not easily read and interpret your facial expressions.
- His facial expressions may be muted and difficult to read.

Our culture prizes eye contact as a sign of being in rapport. Parents often tell their children to *"look me in the eye when I'm talking to you."* We feel we are being listened to when there is eye contact.

Many boys and men are uncomfortable with direct eye contact. Think back to the Hunters…if a hunted animal looked them in the eye, it was a threat.

When you insist on eye contact, especially when he is stressed, you are triggering the 'Fight or Flight' response, which means an infusion of cortisol, adrenaline and testosterone.

Conversely, when he is engaged in conflict, making eye contact shows he is in an aggressive mode!

Notice what men prefer to do together…watch sports, work on cars, play cards…they are shoulder-to-shoulder, relating together with an object 'out there.' Many women have told me that they've had the best conversations with their partners in the car. He is driving (physically active), his eyes are on the road and he is shoulder-to-shoulder with her, bypassing the need for eye contact.

He is listening even if he isn't looking into your eyes. And he may even be able to listen better if his hands are busy, too. Yes, it is important to teach your boy to establish and maintain eye contact. Realizing that it is difficult when he is under stress is the key.

Voice Tone

- He feels your voice tone before he hears your words.
- Use your breath (see the following exercise) to give your voice authority without sounding angry or out of control.
- Practice breath control so you will be able to speak calmly when the situation is stressful.
- Express your disapproval with 'I' statements and then return to your warm, loving voice tone.

Words

- Less is more. Your excessive requests, questions and opinions overwhelm and confuse him. (Remember the *"Waa, waa, waah"* of the adults in the Charlie Brown cartoons?)
- Practice one or two word requests and be prepared to follow through.

- Make your request specific.

- Adding an *"Okay?"* to the end of a request negates your authority.

- Be careful with labels. Label the behavior, rather than the boy. Change: *"You are so messy"* (which labels him), to: *"Your toys are still on the floor"* (which describes what you see).

- Even positive labels can be confusing. Use sparingly.

Your Breath communicates your calm

Animals who breathe the slowest live the longest. Elephants are slow, deep breathers in comparison to mice. The healthful effects of slowed breathing coupled with a calm mind have been well-documented.

To stay calm and speak with authority, rather than anger, practice the following breathing exercise…

1. Place hands palm down across your belly button. Imagine you are floating a little toy boat, up and down, on your belly.

2. Slowly breathe in through your nose on a count of 3, filling your lungs with air.

3. Hold for count of 3 and release through your mouth completely for a count of 3.

4. Pause for a count of 3 and breathe in again – low and deep.

5. After 3 deep breaths, say out loud, *"How are you today?"* Note how it sounds and how it feels to speak those words.

6. Now, shift your hands up to the bony part of your chest, laying palms flat.

7. Bring your breath into this upper part of your body. It is sometimes difficult to do when we intend to, although our breath is often here when we aren't thinking about it.

8. Take 3 breaths, keeping air high and shallow, and then speak out loud, *"How are you today?"*

9. What differences in sound and feeling did you notice?

10. Return to deep breathing and practice until it becomes a habit.

Your Thoughts

We have over 50,000 thoughts each day! Are your thoughts positive or negative? How are you thinking about your boy? Change your thoughts and you'll find other changes happening, too.

Dr. Susan Johnson (www.youandyourchildshealth.org) explains that, biologically, what we think, *"determines the kinds of hormones and neurological transmitters that are secreted within our body. If we hold onto our anger and do not find a way to transform it, these 'thoughts' of anger become secretions that determine our moods.*

If we continually 'live' in a state of anger or sadness then our emotions can actually affect our physical body (our posture, the way we walk, the lines on our face, our voice), and depending upon the strength of our immunity, these emotional states can suppress our immune system and lead to physical illness."

"Thought is a vital, living force, the most vital, subtle and irresistible force there is in the universe. The spoken word is nothing more…than the outward expression of our thoughts. Every thought you entertain is a force that goes out, and every thought comes back laden with its kind."
~Ralph Waldo Trine, 1899
" In Tune with the Infinite"

What thoughts can you begin to change?

Psychogeography

A big word which simply means:
the effect that location has upon the interaction.

Many parents have found that this single concept has the most positive effect on their communication and the response they get from their children.

Psychogeography Practice

Do this exercise with an adult partner. Speaking this nonsense phrase in a neutral voice puts the focus on <u>body language</u> rather than voice tone or word meaning.

"Apples, pears, bananas."

In each of the following positions:

- Speak the neutral phrase
- Take a deep breath between each interaction
- P = Parent, who is the speaker
- C = Child, who is the listener

1. P faces C about 1 foot apart. P says: *"Apples, pears, bananas."*

2. P faces C standing about 10 feet apart. P speaks phrase.

3. C turns away from P (still 10 feet apart). P speaks phrase.

4. P stands shoulder-to-shoulder with C (facing in the same direction). P has hand on C's shoulder. P speaks phrase.

5. C squats down (to about 3 feet) while facing P. P speaks phrase.

6. P squats down while facing C. P speaks phrase.

Before discussing, switch roles and repeat the exercise.

NLP exercise adapted, with thanks, from Lindagail Campbell

What did you notice?

1. Which positions were comfortable for you?

2. Which positions felt less comfortable?

3. When was it easier to listen?

4. When was it easier to ignore the speaker?

Consider your Parenting Psychogeography

1. When your requests are most effective, where are you located in relation to your boy?

2. Where are you located when you make requests that you have to repeat?

3. How often do you give directions or make requests from another room?

4. How often do you talk to your boy when <u>your</u> back is turned? When <u>his</u> back is turned?

5. Note for yourself which interactions are least effective and re-run the scenario through your mind, changing your psychogeography. How does the situation change?

Fundamentals

These subtle, yet profound, tools for understanding our fellow humans provide you with more flexibility and compassion in any interaction. Use them in all of your relationships!

You'll find more communication skills to enhance your quality of life by researching Neuro-Linguistic Programming (NLP).

"Wisdom is knowing what to do when."
~John Grinder

Meanwhile…keep lovin' your boy!

11. Gender Differences

As you begin, thank yourself for taking the time to understand and practice some basics of communication. How will you adjust your expectations and your communication with your boy? How will these insights influence your other relationships?

Take a moment to do that now...

Exploring Gender Differences

One of the many fascinating books exploring gender differences is *Why Gender Matters,* by Dr. Leonard Sax. An advocate for single sex education, he highlights scientific research that sheds light on crucial differences between genders.

He emphasizes that... *Gender differences in childhood are larger and more important than gender differences in adulthood.*

Yes, gender does matter…at home…and even more at school!

But is anyone paying attention?

Hearing Differences

Dr. Sax reports on a study of adults humming the Brahms lullaby over and over to premature babies as musical therapy. The girl babies were able to be discharged, on average, 12 days earlier than girl babies who were not hummed to.

There was *no* difference, however, among the baby boys because the boys *did not even hear the higher frequency humming!* The study concludes that females hear a *wider range of sounds* than males.

What does this mean for your boy? If he has a soft-spoken female teacher (or mom) and is showing signs of inattention, perhaps it is because he isn't hearing her soft voice!

Dr. Sax says…

> *Some boys diagnosed with ADD may just need the teacher to raise her voice a bit.*

Profound, isn't it?

Furthermore, Steve Biddulph, in *Raising Boys,* reports that when 11-13 year old boys experience a rapid growth spurt, their ear canals are affected. As the ear canal stretches, thins and often blocks up, he may have some temporary hearing loss. Make sure your boy hears you by checking in with a light touch on the shoulder and making brief eye contact.

Crying Differences

Michael Gurian reports on the difference between the structure of male and female tear glands. He explains that women have higher levels of prolactin, resulting in larger tear glands. So, even in a tear-friendly culture, you'll see fewer tears falling from a male's eyes.

Differences in Art

According to Dr. Sax, young girls typically draw symmetrical pictures of people, pets, flowers and trees. They prefer the warmer colors: red, orange, green and beige. They use, on average, 10 or more colors in their pictures.

Young boys typically draw action – planes shooting flames, robots attacking, and aliens eating each other. They prefer the cooler colors:

black, gray, silver and blue. They typically use only about 6 colors in their drawings. (I once had a boy in my class who used only brown for an entire school year!)

Teachers have been trained to encourage children to draw colorful pictures with a focus on people and relationships. Feedback from an unaware teacher or parent may give boys the subtle message that their drawings are somehow not okay.

Parents and teachers need to accept 'gross' from boys. Otherwise, boys soon figure out that 'art is for girls' and, once again, they may feel disconnected from the school experience.

A familiar gender dilemma...which toy?

We used to think that if boys were given dolls to play with, they would learn to be more nurturing and if girls were given trucks to play with, they would learn to be more physical and tough.

Well, research has confirmed what parents of both boys and girls have already figured out...give a boy a doll and he'll play with it *much differently* than a girl.

Dr. Jane Healy, in *Your Child's Growing Mind*, quoted a mom of 5 year old twins...

> *"I'm doing my best to raise them in a 'nonsexist' environment, but G. spends a lot of time playing 'house' with her friends, and B. only wants to build things and run around the neighborhood. No matter how much I encourage them toward other activities, they seem to be stereotyping themselves!"*

Both boys and girls benefit from toys that are 'open-ended'. If you give a child a fire truck, complete with ladders and bells, that toy can only be a fire truck. But if you give a child a simply-formed wooden block with wheels, that toy can become a fire truck, a space ship, a boat or an ambulance!

Providing toys that spark the imagination and allowing ample time for his free play is the best early education you can give your boy.

Albert Einstein, who had many hours of free play as a child said...

> *"The greatest scientists are artists as well. Imagination is more important than knowledge. Knowledge is limited. Imagination circles the world."*

And while you are considering *what kind* of toys…consider simplifying his toy collection, too! Kim John Payne, in *Simplicity Parenting,* states that the average child has over 150 toys! That's overwhelming for an adult! Imagine how overwhelming (and stressful) it is for your child. Too many choices and too much 'stuff' is stressful for your boy! Simplify!

Still not convinced? In a study of why siblings fight, reported in *Nurture Shock,* the most common reason cited was sharing toys. Almost 80% of older children, and 75% of younger children, said sharing possessions and claiming them as their own, caused the most fights.

As gender differences continue to be revealed, it is imperative that we educate ourselves and share with others…

so that all children are nurtured for their unique qualities.

Meanwhile…keep lovin' your boy!

12. The Brain – His and Hers

As you begin, take a moment to thank yourself for noticing the different ways your boy operates in the world. If you are female, have you experimented with changing the volume of your speaking voice?

Take a moment to do that now...

The Human Brain

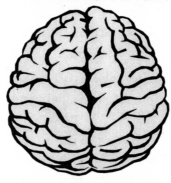

The brain is the only organ that can contemplate itself.

Weighing in at three pounds, the brain is soft and jelly-like, comprised of 80% water. It uses 20% of the oxygen we breathe and the calories we consume. The inside of the bony skull has ridges and sharp protrusions pointing in towards the soft brain matter.

A slight cushion of fluid protects the brain from the skull and gives it buoyancy. However, this cushion is not enough to fully protect the fragile brain. When a head is hit, the brain slams against the skull and little blood vessels on the surface of the brain burst, causing scar tissue to develop.

Brain Health

Dr. Daniel Amen, (www.amenclinics.com), and his team have conducted over 38,000 brain scans using SPECT scan technology. An expert on the brain, he considers these areas essential for optimal brain health:

- **Proper nutrition** – Include lots of protein and water and limit sugar. Protein for breakfast will help your boy 'settle into' his day.

- **Limiting screen time** – Rapid movement, vivid action and sedentary viewing affect the brain's ability to grow itself in a healthy way.

- **Preventing brain injuries** – Injuries tend to accumulate over time. Notice any changes in behavior (often subtle) that may arise after a head injury. Brain injuries can occur without a loss of consciousness. In fact, Amen reports that undiagnosed brain injuries number over one million in the United States.

Because your boy has a natural tendency to take risks, it is imperative that you take steps to safe-guard his brain in these boy-favorite activities…

Sports

- Head-butting a soccer ball puts him at risk for compromised concentration, memory and judgment. (Amen cites a US study that showed *"attention and concentration deficits were significantly more common among those who 'headed' the ball most often."*)

- Discourage football. (Amen cites a Virginia Tech study that fitted player's helmets with air-bag sensors and found that *"players are struck in the head thirty to fifty times per game and regularly endure blows similar to those experienced in car crashes."*)

- Make helmets for all sports <u>non-negotiable</u>! (Biking & skate boarding included).

What is the best sport? Amen states that *"Golf is good. Tennis is terrific. Table tennis is the world's best sport! Football, boxing and soccer are bad for the brain."* He continues, *"As a society, we need to seriously rethink what we allow our children to do…Brain injuries can interrupt, delay, or alter social and intellectual development, sometimes seriously."*

Media

Children believe that *everything* they see and hear is real. If you say you are *'feeling blue'* he will wait for you to turn blue! As a teen, he will begin to develop the ability to discern, make abstractions, and filter input. (This is why sarcasm is lost on children.)

Research has shown that exposure to media:

- Decreases attention span

- Increases aggressive behavior

- Increases obesity

- Increases symptoms of fatigue and stress

- Shows children relational stereotypes which affect their real world relationships

Proceed with caution!

Video Games

Brain scans have shown that when a person is playing video games, the pleasure center in the brain lights up. This is the *same area that lights up when using cocaine,* making addiction a real possibility. Remember those seizures in children watching *Pokémon* in Japan? Dr. Amen states, *"Video games trigger sub-clinical seizures in vulnerable children and adults, causing behavior and learning problems."*

He continues, *"There is no long-term value to playing video games. They actually train the brain to need more and more stimulation to focus, heightening overall stress levels."*

Have you noticed that boys are most susceptible to the lure of video games? Again, proceed with caution!

His Fragile Brain

The Y chromosome is responsible for this fragility at a cellular level. Obstetrical nurses can tell you that birth complications are twice as common in boys. In school, seven boys for every one girl are diagnosed with 'learning disorders.' And interestingly, males have a higher rate of the diseases that affect self-control such as: Tourette's, schizophrenia, autism and drug-alcohol addictions.

We need to protect the *neural* fragility of boys,
Just as we naturally protect the *physical* fragility of girls.

Her Brain

In an effort to help husbands and wives understand each other, marriage guru and humorist, Mark Gungor (www.laughyourway.com) has likened the female brain to a ball of wire or the internet superhighway – always on, moving at a rapid-fire pace, connecting past to present, present to future, and future to past, and talking about the people, places, emotions and events involved - all at the same time!

His Brain

The male brain, on the other hand, Gungor explains, is like a series of boxes. Each box contains one topic: food, sex, sports, sex, and biggest of all: THE NOTHING BOX. Men like the Nothing Box!

The differences become clearer…

> *A young man told me, "My girlfriend talks all the time! She worries about things that haven't even happened yet! I just want to eat my dinner."*

Only about 25% of the male brain is engaged while in a resting state, compared to the female brain, with more than 50% of the brain engaged. The female brain is always on in contrast to the male brain that, as one man told me, *"decides to think about something."* [Or nothing]!

A friend told me, "*I wake up in the morning with lists of things to do running through my mind. My husband says he just wakes up thinking about how hungry he is!* "

Most men would agree that *she never stops thinking,* which may mean that she *never stops talking,* too!

When you think back to the qualities the Hunter needed, his brain adapted to turning on fast and expending energy in quick bursts. His brain evolved to need stimuli to get it fired up and then *it needed time to rest and re-charge.* This is still true today.

After his brain rests...then, *and only then,* can he re-connect with you!

So how does the male brain rest? You've seen it...think about the old man in the fishing boat...there he sits all day, not catching a fish but as content as can be! Or it may be Dad coming home and wanting to nap, go for a run, or play a video game before he is ready to engage in family life.

When women understand that men and boys need time to:

Rest and Recharge in order to Re-Connect

will their behavior be viewed with more acceptance and less frustration?

One woman said...

> *"Now I get it! Now I don't feel like he is ignoring or rejecting me...I just know he needs a break."*

When teachers know this, how will they respond to the boy who is absentmindedly fidgeting with his pencil or staring out the window?

Bridge Brains

Scientists have discovered that brains are not purely male or female; the differences fall on a continuum. Those closest to the middle are called Bridge Brains. This means some boys may show more female-brain tendencies (such as the ability to multi-task easily) and conversely, some girls may show more male-brain tendencies (such as heightened spatial abilities).

Practically Speaking...about his brain

While the male brain is 25% larger overall, there are 25% *less* connecting nerves between the right and left hemispheres of the brain, which means:

- He has <u>fewer</u> places to process your words. Use *visual cues* instead.

- He will have a <u>slower response time</u> to your requests, sometimes as long as 60 seconds! *Be patient.*

- He is <u>easily overwhelmed </u>by too many words. *Use one word requests.* *Wait between requests.*

Boys have 15% *more* spinal fluid, which means:

- Messages <u>move rapidly</u> between the brain and the body. Expect external responses.

- He has <u>less ability</u> to stop and consider the consequences of his actions.

- His reactions may be <u>physical and abrupt</u>!

Reflections on how your Boy responds

1. How do your boy's responses align (or not) with those above?

2. Does your boy have a bridge brain? What qualities does he show to lead you to this conclusion?

3. How can you begin to adjust your expectations of your boy?

> *"You only need a brain when you are moving.*
> *For stationary life forms a brain is no longer needed."*
> ~Susan Greenfield

Meanwhile...keep lovin' your boy!

13. Testosterone *Drives the Bus!*

As you begin, take a moment to thank yourself for noticing how the environment may or may not support the physical needs of your boy. And thank yourself for beginning to make adjustments in your expectations of boys and men as you learn more about their essential nature.

Take a moment to do that now…

"What's testosterone got to do with it?!"

It is risky to over-generalize about boys and girls, and men and women, yet science has proven over and over that males and females *really are different!* And testosterone is a primary reason for that difference!

More than just a growth hormone, testosterone affects mood and energy. It produces boisterous, energetic behavior and a desire for competition. It boosts self-confidence and single-mindedness, as well as the desire to take risks.

Recognizing, nurturing and valuing the testosterone-driven qualities in boys and men is essential to understanding them!

Testosterone before Birth

Did you know that for the first seven weeks after conception, boys and girls are actually the same?! When the Y chromosome awakens, testosterone starts being made and the fetus becomes a boy. By 15 weeks, in utero, the testicles are fully developed and make even more testosterone.

Testosterone through the Years

Steve Biddulph, in *Raising Boys,* explains the role that testosterone plays throughout life...

At birth - A boy has as much testosterone as he will have at age 12!

Two months after birth – His testosterone tapers off and remains the same as girls throughout the toddler years.

Age 4 - A surge at this age brings levels to nearly double. This leads to increased interest in action, adventure and vigorous play.

Age 5 - Testosterone levels drop by half and stay similar to girls.

Age 11-13 - Levels rise sharply (eventually to 800% more than toddler levels!) and the boy's entire system needs to 'rewire' itself to accommodate this sudden growth. As arms and legs elongate, boys of this age tend to be temporarily disorganized and forgetful.

Age 14 - Levels reach their peak, muscle mass increases and voices change. Sexual feelings, restlessness and risk-taking urges are strong. IQ is also affected – boys catch up with girls in written and verbal ability and surge ahead in mathematical ability.

Mid-20s - While testosterone levels remain high, his body has adjusted to it. Surges of creative energy, love of competition, desire to achieve and to be protective can be channeled into activities and career choices that will bring life-long satisfaction.

The 40s - Levels begin to decline, although there is still enough to endow him with high cholesterol, baldness and hairy ears! He has less to prove and mellows into quiet leadership, steady friendships and may even go for days without thinking about sex!

Testosterone through the Day

Michael Gurian, in *Leadership and the Sexes,* notes that men have a daily testosterone cycle and it is helpful to understand how this hormone influences men in different ways throughout the day…

Morning – Men experience a surge upon waking.

9 – 11 a.m. – Further surges mean men are inclined to be more aggressive, ambitious and determined, with a feeling of confidence and a competitive edge.

3 – 5 p.m. – Lower levels mean men tend to be more agreeable to suggestions, less aggressive and less defensive.

Evening – Testosterone rises again but lowers around 8 p.m. Oxytocin, the 'tend and befriend' hormone, rises and men are more likely to talk about their feelings and resolve conflicts, if the conflicts are not too large.

Understanding this may help you to pace your conversations as you begin to notice how the daily cycle of testosterone influences male behavior.

Practically Speaking…what he needs

Physical First - Always!

- With less blood flow to the brain, boys need physical movement to 'wake up' their brains for academic learning.

- He'll be more able to talk about his feelings if he moves first.

- Squeezing a ball, drawing, ripping paper or playing with beeswax while talking (and listening) allows a release of testosterone and enables him to process words more readily.

Expressing Feelings

- Aggression – Nurturance. Boys often express themselves physically in a way that can be uncomfortable and surprising to others. Karate kicks and wrestling are as bonding to boys as chatting over the latest social happening or fashion magazine is for girls.

- Help him increase his emotional vocabulary by describing feelings and reactions and point out the impact of his actions on others.

- Translate his feelings into *thinking* rather than asking him how he *feels*. Rather than, *"How did that make you feel?"* Try: *What did you think about that?"*

- Justice is important. Boys need and want clear rules. Make them and enforce them evenhandedly. Boys can then relax and drop their 'tough-guy' acts.

'Driving the Bus'...

- The power of testosterone can feel overwhelming. Men - Dads, uncles, teachers, friends – are the ones who must take responsibility for teaching boys how to 'stop the bus.'

- Male emotions often default to anger. Men are the ones who must teach, both explicitly and by example, other ways of expressing complex emotions.

- Teaching boys that bodies are to be respected means that they learn: *"No means No" and "Stop means Stop"*. This is non-negotiable.

- Learning self-control means slowing reaction time. Teach breath control and other acceptable ways of calming down.

- Acknowledge boys when they choose thinking and speaking before reacting.

- Story allows talking about feelings in an indirect, often more comfortable way. Relate stories from your own childhood or even frame a story with, *"There was once this kid…"* or something similar.

Two more influential Hormones

Cortisol – the 'Fight or Flight' hormone

When your boy is stressed, cortisol and adrenaline are released into his system causing a 'Fight or Flight' reaction. Even more testosterone is secreted, too, causing his brain to say: *"Be assertive! Be aggressive! Interrupt now! Take risks!"* [Conversely, when females are stressed and their cortisol levels rise, more oxytocin is secreted which causes them to bond even more and compete even less.]

> *The cortisol that is flooding his system can be diluted within 5 minutes…simply by drinking water!*

Stress takes many forms:

- media and video games
- environmental stress

- family and relationship stress
- being asked to move from task to task quickly

Good and Bad Stress

Good stress motivates us to thrive. The stress of challenging a 'personal best' at sports or in academics helps us to be better than we think we can be.

Bad stress, which can be either traumatic or continual, causes the body to 'raise the stress-bar' higher and higher, not allowing itself to reset to a relaxed state. This stress has long-term, harmful effects.

Oxytocin – the 'Tend and Befriend' hormone

Bonding with her newborn, a mother's system is flooded with oxytocin. This hormone is the glue of social bonding. Female oxytocin levels rise when they talk with each other.

Males naturally have less oxytocin, which makes them slower to respond to others with empathy. They are also less likely to see how their behavior impacts their relationship with others. Adults need to be explicit with boys: *"When you hit your brother, he will not want to play with you."*

Understanding the role of testosterone and other hormones in your boy's life is yet another key to shaping a supportive, compassionate and nurturing environment for him.

For more about boys and testosterone see...

Raising Boys by Steve Biddulph. Why boys are different – and how to help them become happy and well-balanced men. Celestial Arts, 1998.

The Good Son (and other titles) by Michael Gurian. Shaping the moral development of our boys and young men. Tarcher/Putnam, 1999.

Why Gender Matters by Dr. Leonard Sax. What parents and teachers need to know about the emerging science of sex differences. Broadway, 2005.

Meanwhile... keep lovin' your boy!

14. The Ages and Stages of His Life

As you begin, thank yourself for taking the time to understand the role that hormones play throughout your boy's life. Thank yourself for adjusting your reactions to your boy, as needed, as you begin to assimilate new ideas into your parenting.

Take a moment to do that now...

Engaging his Head, his Heart and his Hands

Since the days of Plato and Aristotle, mankind has sought ways to categorize human development in an effort to understand the complex beings that we are.

In his book, *Understanding Waldorf Education,* Jack Petrash notes that Rudolf Steiner designed Waldorf education, *"around the simple idea that children have within them three fundamental forces impelling them toward physical, emotional, and mental activity."*

As children develop, they must be engaged in three distinct areas:

Head   *Heart*   *Hands*

> *"He who works with his hands is a laborer.*
>
> *He who works with his hands and his head is a craftsman.*
>
> *He who works with his hands and his head and his heart is an artist."*
>
> St. Francis of Assisi

While we develop our hands, our head, and our hearts continually as we grow, each stage demands a certain focus in order to fully blossom.

Developing the Hands - The Age of Imitation

> *"It is through our inner attitude that we show our love. It's not just what we do; it's who we are in the doing of the things, that speaks to our child."*
> Sharifa Oppenheimer, Heaven on Earth

Ages 0-7 - What you DO is most important...

Action, activity, and more action! Exploration of the world at this age is a full-body experience! He is exploring the world with every sense. He learns everything from language to how to dress and eat by *imitating* those around him.

Young children experience the world without reservation, with no ability to filter what is <u>good</u> to imitate and what is <u>bad</u> to imitate.

As Petrash explains, *"Young children imitate far more than we imagine and the impressions they take in and mimic become behaviors that are learned for life."*

What are you giving him to imitate? What are you modeling as you move through your daily life? Are you hurried and short-tempered? Are you calm and even-keeled?

Are you helping him learn to engage in meaningful work by showing him the way? Are you providing him with quality tools to do his work? A child-sized broom, a basin of warm water and soap for dishwashing at his height and shelves for putting toys away all contribute to establishing life-long habits.

The Importance of Play

> *"Play is the work of childhood."*
> ~ *Ashley Montague*

Free, unstructured play is the core of childhood. Children process their thoughts and feelings through their play. Researchers continue to confirm that through imaginative play and active movement, children develop the foundation needed for later academic success.

Sharifa Oppenheimer, in *Heaven on Earth,* suggests that when his play goes awry and he is out of sorts, bring him closer to you and guide him into your rhythm as you calmly go about your day. Time-outs then become 'time-ins' and he feels embraced rather than abandoned.

It may take longer to accomplish your tasks but the habits you are instilling are providing a strong foundation for his future self-discipline. In this age of activity and imitation, you need to <u>show</u> him the way to behave, rather than pleading or bargaining with him.

Understanding that he does not yet have the cognitive reasoning to decide to 'be bad' nor can he think through the consequences of his actions means that *do-over's* are an effective teaching tool. Staying neutral and calm are your tasks as you show him the way.

Practically Speaking…a note about child care

If your boy is in a day care setting, does it also give him images and moods worthy of his imitation? Is the day care provider worthy of his imitation and reverence?

Steve Biddulph, in *Raising Boys,* cautions against a large childcare setting for your boy under the age of 3.

Biddulph says, *"Many studies have shown that boys are more prone than girls to separation anxiety and to becoming emotionally shut down as a result of feeling abandoned. Also, a boy of this age can develop restless or aggressive behavior in childcare and carry this label, and the role that goes with it, right on into school."*

Choosing a loving relative or family daycare is much more appropriate for young boys. He concludes, *"The first lessons boys need to learn are closeness, trust, warmth, fun and kindness. Children under three need to spend the long days of childhood with people to whom they are very special."*

> *"Young children are very busy. Their evolution in the first ten years of life – neural, social, and physical – makes what we do as adults look like standing still."* ~K. Payne, Simplicity Parenting

Developing the Heart - The Age of Emotional Expansion

> *"The salvation of the human world lies nowhere else than the human heart."*
> ~Vaclav Havel

Ages 7-14...What you FEEL is most important...

You are the guide now, interpreting and expanding his social and emotional awareness. You are the interpreter of the impact of his actions and decisions. Direct is best. He wants to know how he messed up. Be clear and specific.

Guide him in how he can be more successful in the future. Avoid asking, *"**Why** did you do that?"* He likely won't have an answer but may not hesitate to make one up! Remember that it is important for you to maintain your calm neutrality as your boy learns and falters along the way.

Boys need time to process their feelings. If pressed, his first instinct will be to blame someone else, a common defense response for males. Give him a few minutes, some water, time outside, then he will be able to return and talk about his feelings.

School age children, especially around the age of nine, begin to recognize their separateness. They realize they have an inner world that no one else has access to. Their feeling life expands and their empathy develops. Taking care of a pet or being of service to others are healthy ways to support this development.

Dad or another father-figure becomes even more important for your boy now, as he begins to study how to be a man. He is watching Dad and other men as he learns to be happy and secure in his maleness. Mom can step back a little more and let Dad come more to the foreground.

Developing the Head - The Age of Thinking

> *"Thought is action in rehearsal."*
> ~Sigmund Freud

Ages 14-21 - What you THINK is most important...

When polled by social scientists, parents said having a teenager at home was very stressful. However, teens, when polled, didn't find adolescence as traumatic. Parents rated arguing destructive, while teens found it to be productive.

When young adults argue, become opinionated or critical, they are increasing their ability to think. Allowing him to fully express his opinions and keeping an open mind is essential to building his self-confidence and relational skills.

Watch for conversational openings on his schedule, which are often late at night or in the car. You may want to doze on your son's bed until he comes home from his evening. Those may be your best conversations of the day!

Young men are looking for input from other men, in addition to Dad. That means grandpa, uncles, mentors and teachers. Parents need to step back and create opportunities for other worthy men to step in. They can lend a steady hand and affirm his goodness (especially when you're having trouble seeing it!). Continuing to learn responsibility and self-respect is part of joining the adult community.

Practically Speaking...more about Teens

Sleep

- Teens need more sleep now than at any time since infancy!

- 60% of high school students report extreme daytime sleepiness.

- Children get an hour less sleep each night than they did 30 years ago. The cost of that lost hour has an exponential impact because children's brains are a work in progress until age 21.

- Many 'typical' teen characteristics can be attributed to chronic sleep deprivation – moodiness, depression and even binge eating.

- In a study reported in *Nurture Shock,* measuring the effect of sleep loss on student test performance, it was found that, *"The loss of one hour of sleep is equivalent to [the loss of] two years of cognitive maturation and development."* That means a slightly sleepy sixth grader will test at a normal fourth grade level.

And More

- Re-wiring of the brain's circuitry may mean his conversation and thoughts are expressed slowly. Be patient.

- Objection to parental authority is typically stronger at age 11 than it is at age 18, peaking around age 14-15.

- Self-concept changes rapidly as he tries on different selves.

- He needs you to be available more than ever before. That means late night chats, picking him up from social gatherings, and taking an interest in his school and friends.

- Keep your refrigerator full of food and welcome all of his friends.

- Read what he reads.

- Encourage him to think through real-life problems and dilemmas. Seek his opinion and be respectful.

- Expect his criticism of you, his school and his teachers. Help him verbalize his opinion and insist on respectful disagreement.

- Be consistent and firm with boundaries. One dad put a padlock on his son's bike when it was off-limits.

- Have dinner together regularly. According to the Center for Addiction and Substance Abuse, *"The more often teens have dinner with their parents, the less likely they are to smoke, drink or use drugs."*

- Insist on down-time. You may not know what is going on with him but if you notice changes or stress, create time for him to pull-back. A weekend away from friends and activities may give him the fresh perspective he needs.

- Teens with Dads who have bonded with them in the first months of their lives are more likely to successfully navigate adolescence.

(Some of the above excerpted from Dr. Jane Healy's book, *Your Child's Growing Mind* and *Nurture Shock* by Po Bronson & Ashley Merryman)

"It all adds up to a hard and rapid falling into earthly life, from which no one can escape without a few bruises!"
~ *Eugene Schwartz*

Meanwhile… keep lovin' your boy!

15. Peer and Adult Influence

Boys will be boys and *Boys need men*

As you begin, thank yourself for taking the time to reflect on the different ages and stages of your boy. What was new? What were you reminded about? What changes can you make that embrace your new knowledge? Does it help you understand other men in your life?

Take a moment to do that now…

'Tough guys'

It may seem, at times, that boys come into this world ready to 'do battle.' It is as if they are already clothed in armor and so the world responds to their 'tough-guy' façade. It seems that the ancient Hunter still remains inside the boy so that he inherently feels that attack is his best defense.

In a paper on gender roles, a 16-year old boy wrote, *"Boys are tough but we get hurt like anyone else. I cry a lot – just not with tears."*

Modeling and teaching boys how to be vulnerable will allow them to discover their own resiliency and will enable them to learn to trust themselves and the world.

The Influence of Peers
and Managing His Risk-Taking Behaviors

In *Why Gender Matters,* Dr. Sax discusses the distinct difference between boys and girls when it comes to risky behavior. He notes that girls and boys *"assess risk differently."*

He says, *"As soon as kids are old enough to toddle across the floor, boys are significantly more likely to do something dangerous: put their fingers in a socket, try to stand on a basketball, jump off a chair onto the floor."*

And, you may have noticed what Dr. Sax confirms, *"When parents try to stop their child from doing something risky, boys are less likely to comply."*

When psychologists interviewed children who have been injured or in 'close calls,' they have found that…

- Boys typically *over-estimate* their own ability.

- Boys were *less likely* to tell their parents about their injuries.

- Boys attributed their injuries *erroneously* to 'bad luck' rather than lack of skill or planning.

- Boys were *more likely* to be around other boys at the time of their injury.

Dr. Sax concludes, *"A boy is much more likely to do something dangerous or stupid when he's in a group of boys than when he is by himself."*

Boys are impressed by other boys who take physical risks. Successfully riding his bike off a 4-foot wall in front of a group of his peers increases his social standing. It also gives him 'a charge,' a release of cortisol (the 'fight or flight' hormone) that makes him feel tingly and excited – an irresistible force!

Dr. Sax knows this is *"a tough concept for some women to grasp. A mother who warns her son, 'Don't ride your bike off the boardwalk. You might get hurt,' has missed the point. Her son knows it's dangerous. He's riding his bike off the boardwalk because it is dangerous."*

Boys are going to take risks. It is important to allow them to 'start small.' When he falls and scrapes his knee as a 3-year old, he learns that he can get hurt and recover. He begins to discover his limits and builds his self-confidence, competence, and resiliency.

How do you let him take risks and still stay safe?

Dr. Sax suggests…

- **Boys in groups do stupid things.** Your boy wants a thrill, so take the whole family skiing or snowboarding, insisting on lessons (and helmets) for all. *"A family trip to the ski slopes is a much safer undertaking than a group of teenage boys going to the same mountain."*

- **Supervised risk is better than unsupervised risk.** Get him involved in activities that have a risky aspect but are supervised – rock climbing, organized sports (no head butting in soccer, no football), or kayaking.

- **Assert your authority.** If you've forbidden an activity, follow up with no negotiation or argument. Dr. Sax gives the example, *"If he's not allowed to ride his mountain bike without your permission, put a steel cable lock on it until you've decided he can ride again – when you know where, when and with whom he'll be riding."*

And, of course, every boy is going to approach risk-taking differently.

Notice whether his risk-taking behavior increases with a certain group of friends and take steps to get them engaged in organized, supervised activities.

Do you see the influence of testosterone?   Can you help him manage it?

> *"The central struggle of parenthood is to let our hopes for our children outweigh our fears."*
> ~ Ellen Goodman

His Moral Development

Historically, young boys have been initiated into adulthood by 'rites of passage.' In recent decades, our society seemed to be losing this impulse for guiding and instructing young men. Now there are many groups that have taken up this important work. Two of them are *Boys to Men* (www.boystomen.org) and *BAM – Boys Advocacy and Mentoring* (www.bamgroups.com).

With a boy's tendency to externalize his responses (and with the extra oomph of testosterone), it is crucial that his physical impulses and risk-taking behavior be managed.

Our ancestors dealt with this by providing times of intense moral and disciplinary development.

Steve Biddulph, in *Raising Boys,* tells of the Native American Lakota tribe's traditional way of guiding boys into manhood. He explains that this native culture was *"vigorous and successful...characterized by especially good relationships between men and women."*

He describes the tribe's ceremony for boys:

At around the age of fourteen, Lakota boys were sent on a 'vision quest'...This involved sitting and fasting on a mountain peak to await a vision or hallucination brought on by hunger. This vision would include a being that would carry messages from the spirit world to guide the boy's life.

As the boy fasted, and trembled alone on the peak, he would hear mountain lions snarl and move in the darkness below him. In fact, the sounds were made by the men of the tribe, keeping watch, to ensure the boy's safety. A young person was too precious to the Lakota to endanger needlessly.

When the young man eventually returned to the tribe, his achievement was celebrated. But from that day, <u>for two whole years,</u> he was not permitted to speak directly to his mother.

Lakota mothers, like the women of all hunter-gatherer groups, were very close and affectionate with their children, and the children often slept alongside them in the women's huts and tents.

The Lakota believed that if the boy spoke to his mother immediately following his entry into manhood, the attraction back into boyhood would be so great that he would 'fall' back into the world of women and never grow up.

After the two years had passed, a ceremonial rejoining of the mother and son took place. By this time, he was a man and able to relate to her as such.

Women have often found this story very moving – it brings both grief and joy. The reward that Lakota mothers gained from this letting go is that they were assured their sons would return as respectful and close adult friends.

Adult Influence

> *"Show boys you trust them and*
> *expect them to become positive men."*
> *~Howard Hiton*

You may have a sense that your partner changed when he became a Dad.

Now, science is tracking the biology of those changes. Michael Gurian, in *Leadership and the Sexes,* cites a Princeton University study showing that the parts of the brain that control his judgment and executive decision-making *"develop more synapses...after the baby is born."*

He explains that the new Dad, *"becomes more wise, more focused on good decisions, on calming down, paying attention, staying on task."* His oxytocin levels rise, too, increasing the bond to his child.

Boys need a Dad

As a boy grows out of infancy, it is important to let Dad begin to provide much of the guidance, companionship and discipline. In many families, Dad may be working long hours and so Mom continues being the primary parent. She thinks she is being the bridge between Dad and son...but be careful...all too often Mom becomes a barrier in the Dad-son relationship.

Absent Dads

If Dad isn't available, Mom needs to find worthy men and help to foster those connections. Studies have shown that boys with absent Dads are more likely to be violent, get hurt, get into trouble and do poorly in school.

Encourage all adults who are around your boy to speak about the qualities they admire in men, noting their character and highlighting how they handle diverse situations.

Practically Speaking... more for Dads to know

- Your boy is watching you all the time, learning to be a man. He watches everything you do and notes everything you say. Your words have ten times more influence than Mom's words!

- Praise him, tell him you are proud of him – give specific examples. Make sure to praise him for <u>who he is,</u> rather than just for <u>what he does.</u>

- Volunteer in his classroom. Read what he is reading.

- Make time with family and your boy a priority.

- Help him find meaningful work and ways to be helpful to others.

- Enjoy him! Have fun, wrestle, laugh and be silly.

- Be affectionate. Be willing to show him your full range of emotions so that he can show you his.

- Tell him stories. Stories about your life, your friends, and your experiences will help him learn how to be a man. Stories allow an indirect (and more comfortable) way to talk about feelings.

- Talk about sports figures, music and movie stars, how they live their lives and what messages they give.

- Give him direct, specific guidance – don't assume he already knows how to behave (or that he remembers!)

R-E-S-P-E-C-T

Eventually, boys will outgrow their mothers physically. It is imperative that Dad and other men are at the forefront of teaching and modeling respect towards women. Any disrespectful behavior or comments towards women must be stopped immediately.

Hopefully, though, he has been a constant witness to men's respectful attitude towards women and he has learned to behave accordingly.

Meanwhile, Mom, it is important for you to uncover any harmful feelings, beliefs and attitudes you have about men. How were you fathered? Do you have any lingering attitudes or beliefs that may affect your interactions with your boy?

Give yourself some time to review your past relationships with males. Reflect on what you've learned – both positive and negative – and how those experiences may be shaping your beliefs, actions and reactions to your son.

Single Moms

There are over 20 million children living in single parent homes. As Mom of a boy, you have the challenging task of being 'tough and soft' ~ often at the same time!

Setting firm rules and following through with consequences, providing plenty of vigorous activity and nurturing with love and tenderness are all up to you. Likely, you are working outside of the home as well. It is a tall order!

Looking to others – relatives, teachers, friends and community partners – is essential. Many would be thrilled to have you ask for their help in guiding your boy. Many 'empty nesters' would enjoy an afternoon at the park with your boy – you have to ask!

As your boy grows older and gets physically bigger, you must manage conflict with him before it gets out of hand. Taking a time out for yourself and coming back to the issue later is more effective than a yelling match.

Let him know that you won't compromise on his safety or his respect of others. Make family a priority.

For more about boys and fathering…

Covering Home by Jack Petrash. Using the metaphor of baseball to discuss fathering. Robins Lane Press, 2000.

The Courage to Raise Good Men by Olga Silverstein. Emphasizes the importance of mothers in developing emotionally healthy sons. Viking 1994.

Raising Cain by Michael Thompson. Thoughtful approach to raising boy's emotional literacy. Ballantine, 2000.

Meanwhile…keep lovin' your boy!

16. Bring Out His Best at School

As you begin, thank yourself for recognizing the significance you have in your boy's life...and also the significance of his peers and how it affects his risk-taking behaviors. And thank yourself for beginning to look at ways you can change his environment and add men to his life that will encourage him, showing him how to be a 'good' man.

Take a moment to do that now...

The Roots of Education

In ancient times, being able to read and write was considered heroic. Only kings and wise men mastered these arts and they were greatly revered. Today, are any 'superheroes' shown reading and writing?!

School became required by law in the United States in 1852. However, long before that, Plato, the Aztecs and the Talmud all wrote of the benefits of a compulsory education.

Boys want their learning to be <u>relevant</u>. And no wonder, when you consider how boys learned before sitting in a classroom was the law.

Boys were active participants in their learning by...

- Hunting and learning the ways to hunt from elder tribesmen
- Planting, harvesting and storing crops
- Acting as pages and squires to knights and lords
- Learning hands-on skills as apprentices
- Caring for livestock and property
- Laboring in fields and factories

How do boys learn today?

Since 1852, boys have been expected to learn within the confines of a school room. And, although mostly men taught boys those valuable, practical skills listed above, today, only 1 in 9 elementary school teachers are men!

In the classroom, boys are expected to sit still, and when they don't, they are considered behavior problems. More boys than girls are sent to the principal's office.

Not a surprise, the school environment is often stressful for boys. When they are stressed they act up, withdraw, get silly or wild, and rebel against the situation ~ which causes more stress for everyone!

Ways to Bring Out His Best at School

Enlist his Teachers

Let's face it, teachers are overwhelmed. However, when parents can encapsulate information for them, they may be more likely to embrace the changes that can help your boy succeed in school.

Michael Gurian, author of *Boys and Girls Learn Differently* and *Strategies for Teaching Boys and Girls,* works with hundreds of schools, teaching educators simple ways to adapt their teaching techniques to meet the unique learning needs of each gender. (www.gurianinstitute.com)

Because many of these concepts are new, teachers have not had the opportunity to learn and incorporate them. Help spread the word!

Your Boy's Age

Boys are typically 1 – 1.5 years behind girls in their verbal and fine motor development. It is crucial that boys be given extra time before entering first grade. Timing your son's entry into first grade so that he'll be an older child in his class will always work to his advantage.

When young boys realize that they can't write or use scissors as easily as girls, and that their work is sloppy, they begin to feel like, *'School isn't for me! School is for girls!'* Their stress level is heightened and to relieve it, they become overly active, noisy or withdrawn.

Your Boy's Physical Needs

Did you notice that all the ways in which boys learned in 'the olden days' included movement? Boy's brains are designed so that movement and learning go hand-in-hand, enhancing memory and understanding.

Practically Speaking… support your active boy

- **Frequent water** – Keep his brain (which is 80% water!) and body hydrated. Cortisol is the 'fight or flight' hormone and is activated when your boy is stressed or frustrated. Drinking water reduces his cortisol level in just 5 minutes.

- **Move before school** – Help your boy be ready for learning by walking or biking to school. If you drive, plan to arrive early and take a run around the block, jump rope or play basketball.

- **Movement breaks** – Encourage the teacher to incorporate movement during the school day. Five minutes of moving to music, stretching, clapping and stamping rhythms, means lengthened attention spans. Some boys need to 'take a walk' during lessons when they get distracted and wiggly. The teacher can send them on an important errand.

- **Boys relate physically** – When boys wrestle or punch each other, they are connecting with each other as deeply as girls do when playing and chatting together. Teachers can more readily accept boy's physical expressions of friendship when they understand the underlying impulse.

- **Understand anger** – When a boy is angry, his verbal circuitry shuts down. He becomes more physical, often cursing. Because boys are more externally focused, he may decide it isn't his problem or will blame it on someone else. Revisit the incident after a cooling-off period and discuss his feelings and the effect of his actions on his relationships.

- **Stand-up desks** – Simply changing desk styles can enhance his ability to learn. Schools with stand-up desks have found that many students prefer standing while working and they stay more awake and alert. Stools are available so they can sit, too.

- **Active free play after school** – Unstructured play time is essential to relieve stress and strengthen his imagination. Be sure your boy has a minimum of scheduled activities so he can be free to explore, imagine, dream, decompress, and rest his brain!

Go Visual

Classrooms are generally geared toward verbal learning. With their slower capacity for processing verbal input, boys are at a disadvantage. Add to that the 1 – 1.5 year lag in verbal skills and you've got a boy who is stressed and feeling left behind. Some boys experience stress even when given a blank piece of paper and told to write!

When teachers supplement their verbal teaching strategies with graphic organizers such as mind maps, storyboards and outlines, they are helping boys synthesize and process their learning visually, which is often their strongest learning system.

Practically Speaking… support him academically

- **Promote reading** - Make sure your teacher provides reading materials that boys love – comic books, books of lists, instruction manuals, baseball card data, picture encyclopedias and dictionaries. Make sure he sees his parents reading. And see www.guysread.com for more encouragement.

- **Draw before writing** - Allowing boys to draw a story before writing it allows teachers and parents to help him add descriptive words.

- **Accept gross and fantasy violence** - Boys love it and it engages them in reading and writing. Steve Biddulph, in *Raising Boys,* explains that a boy's *'fantasy violence'* (the scenes he plays in his head) is often less gory than what is portrayed in media and video games. Boys need to know that it is okay to express what is inside them and that they can work through it by expressing it with acceptance from adults. The actual 'real' violence that is in the media and video games often disturbs boys with its bloodiness and destruction.

- **Sleep** – Tired children can't process or remember what they've learned. The more he learns during the day, the more sleep he needs at night. Minimum eight hours, ten is better.

Relevance

Boys need their learning to matter, just as in the 'olden days.' Be familiar with his strengths and passions, interests and talents. Watch for places to incorporate them into the curriculum.

My 9th grade neighbor excitedly told me about the bike mechanic class he was taking as an elective. The best part for him was being able to go downtown and help cyclists with bike repairs! His learning just got connected to the real world and his enthusiasm was soaring!

A report about the gender divide in education, sponsored by the *Maine Boys Network 2008,* found that boys, *"loved to discover that they shared a hobby with a teacher, male or female."* They connected their learning ability and liking of the subject to who the teacher was and their relationship with that teacher. *"They want teachers to care about them."*

The report continued…

"In the end, it seems that boys want the same kind of schooling we want for them. They want an engaging curriculum delivered by caring teachers who have faith in them, behave fairly, and adapt their teaching to the different styles of their students."

Boys relayed their feelings about school…

Boys do not like being watched; sitting still for long periods; doing busywork…and feeling time limits/time pressure.

Boys do like having input into the curricula in their classes; participating in kinesthetic, hands-on and investigative activities; seeing connections between what they are learning and their lives outside of school.

Boys also value a positive, fun, laid-back atmosphere in the classroom and the opportunity to try multiple approaches to solving problems.

How does your boy's class measure up? Is his unique learning style being met? Consider how you can support positive changes in his classroom and school.

When the school environment can be adapted to meet him, rather than expecting him to fit into an ill-suited environment, he thrives and feels school is a worthy place for him.

> *"Boys will thrive at school if there is a pervasive sense that they are welcome, that they are liked, and that who they really are – and how they really enjoy learning – will be embraced in a genuine way by their teachers."*
>
> ~ *Dr. W. Pollack,*
> *"Real Boys"*

Meanwhile… keep lovin' your boy!

17. Bring Out His Best at Home

As you begin, thank yourself for considering how your boy's school environment and teacher meet his learning needs. Think about how you can bring ideas for change to school in a respectful and considerate way.

Take a moment to do that now...

Enjoy his Energy!

Boys are energetic and enthusiastic and sometimes seem bigger than the home that holds them! Appreciating your son's masculinity and creating an environment that will nurture it in a positive way reduces stress and increases your enjoyment of his exuberance!

Matching his energy is easiest when you are feeling rested and relaxed. Jam-packed schedules, irregular meal times, and bed times add chaos and stress to his life and yours.

Your Self-Care

When you are well-rested and feeling nurtured, you are able to be 'on your game' as a parent. Don't your children deserve that from you?

When you feel like it's too hard to find the time to take care of yourself, remember, you are showing your boy how to be an adult…and how to be a father to your grandchildren!

- **Breath is the foundation** of your inner (and outer) calm. Remember to breathe deep and low into your belly. Practice soon becomes habit.

- **Staying neutral is essential.** State clearly how you feel about the problem or his behavior, using 'I' statements. Make sure your statements are about the problem or behavior, rather than about him. Ask for his collaboration. Then, move through it, and return to your warm, loving parent-self.

- **Mind your stress**, which can actually shrink your brain! Meditation and exercise strengthen your brain and your ability to counteract stress.

Less is More

Less words. Less questions. Less requests.

- **The more you ask, the less he'll say.** Use fewer words and give him time to respond (up to 60 seconds!) Give him time between your requests. Use gestures rather than words. Post written rules.

- **Silence is golden.** Be comfortable with it. Not everything needs to be analyzed and discussed (save that for your girlfriends, Mom!). A man once told me he feels closer to guys he plays sports with and doesn't really talk to. Share a common activity together, enjoy the quiet companionship. Find something to do side-by-side and you may find that conversation will more easily flow but don't push it.

- **Write it down.** A friendly reminder on his mirror, a note in his lunch box. Be specific in your praise, describing exactly what you noticed, and how it made you feel. *"I saw you help your brother with his backpack this morning. That freed me up to get the car ready to go. Thanks for doing that without being asked!"*

- **"Hmmm…."** Sometimes a curious and interested, "Hmm…" from you is enough. He may just need to say something and really doesn't need (or want) a response from you, he just wants to know you've listened.

Adapt your Home

When the environment suits your boy, you may find he is more relaxed and you are too! Viewing your home through your boy's eyes may reveal areas that could benefit from a change.

Outside Time

Lots of outside time is crucial for boys to process their feelings and release excess energy. Make sure they have a safe place to play and let them go!

I recently visited a friend's beach house and the entire back yard had been turned into a giant fantasy land complete with moats, islands and bridges. Let creative play rule the day!

Inside Time

Your boy will be most comfortable with an uncluttered place to play, allowing him to use his creative ingenuity and release his excess energy.

- **Stow your antiques.** When he is grown you can bring them out again.

- **Install a hanging bar** across a doorway. Tie a long, strong cloth around it. This hammock can be a climbing structure as well as a cozy place to sit. It satisfies both large muscle movement and the need for touch.

- **Mini-trampolines** allow an acceptable energy release. You may find that he likes to bounce and talk to you at the same time!

- **Squeeze balls release energy** while helping him keep his body still. He will be able to listen even better because his hands are busy.

- **Uncluttered play space** with lots of room to spread out his open-ended toys will encourage his imaginative play.

- **Adjust your expectations** of his behavior. Remember that *'every behavior is useful in some context'* and look for the benefits of his exuberance.

- **Limit media.** Boys are easily susceptible to overstimulation.

Enlist Him

Invite him to be a full participant in family life and decision making.

- **Problem solving** - When there is a problem, state it clearly and neutrally. Ask him to help you find a solution. Boys are creative and innovative and he may have a solution you wouldn't have thought of! Acknowledge his feelings while limiting his behaviors.

- **Boys need rules** - Boys crave structure and security. When he has a structure he can count on, he can relax. Boys want to know...

  o   Who is in charge?

  o   What are the rules?

  o   Will the rules be fairly and consistently enforced?

- **Meaningful work** - Boys thrive on meaningful work. Just as he seeks relevance in his learning, he wants to know that his work is useful. For instance, as young as 3, give him the job of putting silverware on the table. You may have to remind him but do not do it for him! When he forgets and the family sits down to dinner without silverware, he will see how important his work is to the family.

- **Responsibility** - The less you do for him, the more responsible he will become. Do not carry his stuff! Help him pack his own lunch. Show him how to do the laundry. You are teaching him habits and your parenting job is about to get a lot easier. Plus, he'll be the envy of his college roommates. And think how happy his future partner will be!

- **Siblings** – The tone that siblings establish with each other (controlling or considerate) stays about the same throughout their lives. Situational studies find that siblings between the ages of 3 and 7 clash about three times per hour. Only 1 of every 8 of those conflicts ends in a compromise or reconciliation. Otherwise, one sibling withdraws while the other 'wins'. Many siblings simply lack the skills of how to initiate play on terms that they can both enjoy and how to graciously decline if they don't want to play. Parents can teach these social skills, allowing siblings to enjoy each other.

Praise – A little goes a long way

The authors of *Nurture Shock* have analyzed recent research and surmise that while 85% of American parents think it is important to tell their children they are smart, all of this praise actually causes children to underperform!

Rather than praising children's intellect, it is important to praise their efforts. Be specific in your praise, *"I like how you tried that math problem again."*

Practically Speaking…praise him effectively

- **Be specific.** Praise his skill or his strategy in ways he can understand.

- **Be sincere.** Children under 7 take praise at face value. Older children become suspicious of too much praise.

- **Excessive praise distorts motivation.** Children do a task to hear the praise rather than for the intrinsic enjoyment they gain.

- **Excessive praise has been shown to make children more competitive.** They must 'tear down' others to maintain their own image.

- **Excessive praise reduces his persistence.** The brain is a muscle and must learn to work through failure and frustration successfully.

- **Include specific strategies for coping with failure.** Gently suggest a different approach.

Making Changes at Home

As you adapt your home environment, it is important to consider what you *do* want, rather than what you *don't* want.

You can do that by asking yourself,

"What do I want instead?"

As you make changes, even little ones, remember that one change leads to more changes. Be sure you've given thought to how the changes you are making will positively or negatively affect others in the family. Is it a change that all can live with?

> "There is no way to be a perfect parent...
> and a million ways to be a good one!"
> ~J. Churchill

Meanwhile...keep lovin' your boy!

18. Now...How do you see your Boy? How do you see Yourself?

Whew! You've been on a long journey. Thank yourself for taking the opportunity to 'walk a mile in his shoes.' And thank yourself for allowing yourself grace in your parenting, even for the mistakes you've made along the way. It is an imperfect science, this parenting...we can only strive and know that our children will love us for the effort that we make!

Take a moment to do that now...

You, Your Boy, and the Curious Observer

Now that you know more about yourself and more about your boy, it is time to revisit the exercise you completed at the beginning of this journey. Only now, you get to add all of the new insights you have gained as you continue to understand the dynamic relationship that exists between you and your boy.

Again, choose an interaction with your boy that...

- Repeats

- Gives you less than satisfactory results

- You would like to change

Again, you get to be the Movie Director of your life!

To begin...

1. Choose a time and place where you will be able to complete this exercise in quiet and without interruption. It will take 20-25 minutes.

2. Ask a partner to read the following script in a warm and loving way. If you would prefer to work alone, you can read the script into a tape and play it back, being sure to leave pauses at the appropriate places (...).

3. Choose an interaction with your boy. Initially, choose an interaction that is fairly mild. Later, repeat this exercise with interactions that are more heated.

4. Stand comfortably, with your eyes closed, so that you can step into the three points of an imaginary triangle: Self, Your Boy, Observer.

5. Your partner reads the following script slowly, pausing with the ellipses (...), and continuing when you've nodded your head to indicate you are ready.

Taking 3 deep breaths...and closing your eyes comfortably...settle yourself into your feet... your knees... your hips...and feeling your own feelings... hearing out of your own ears... seeing out of your own eyes...prepare to rerun a movie of your chosen situation from your own experience...

Begin the movie just before the situation became difficult or awkward... Run the movie from your point of view... seeing what you saw... hearing what you heard... feeling what you felt...

Just viewing the movie... without judgment or criticism... just noticing...

[Pause here while the movie 'runs', wait for a nod]

And when you are ready… take a deep breath and move into the position of your boy…

And settle yourself into feeling like your boy… How is his posture?...What are his gestures?...Move your body…your arms…your legs… so that you can get the feeling of how it is to be your boy in this interaction…

See out of your boy's own eyes… hear out of your boy's own ears…feel what your boy is feeling…and see that 'you over there' out of your boy's own eyes…

As you begin to run the movie again…

Notice what that 'you over there' is doing...how that 'you over there' is sounding… just notice… free of judgment… take in any new learning you might have from this position of being your boy…and seeing that 'you over there'…

[Pause here while the movie 'runs', wait for a nod]

And when you are ready… take a deep breath … as you step into the position of the observer…

This is a place of interested, loving curiosity…as you observe that 'you over there' and 'your boy over there' interacting with each other…

Go ahead and run the movie again… This time taking careful notice of the interplay between that 'you over there' and 'your boy over there'…

Staying free of judgment…being open to new insights and observations… continue to observe the movie to its logical end…

[Pause here while the movie 'runs', wait for a nod]

And when you are ready… take a deep breath… and return to the position of yourself…feeling your own feelings… seeing through your own eyes… and hearing through your own ears…That's right….Good…

And now take a moment to thank yourself for participating in this exercise…acknowledging any new information and insights…as you open your eyes…and return to this room.

Thank your script reader for participating with you.

Now, take some quiet time to reflect on your new experience in each position...

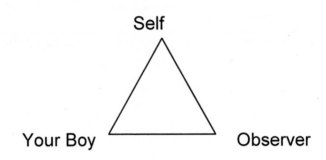

1. How did each position feel this time? Did you notice any changes?

2. What new awareness did you have in the position of 'Your Boy'?

3. What new awareness did you have in the curious, interested 'Observer' position?

4. What new information have you gained from your own point of view?

5. How can you apply that information to the situation the next time?

Congratulations!
You have created a new way of being with your boy.

A New You!

Do you find yourself responding to the *'same old thing'* in a new way?

Do you feel more empathy towards yourself and your boy? Do you have more resourceful ways of responding to your boy?

Remember, when you practice *'stepping into someone else's shoes'* you gain new flexibility, understanding and choices in *all* of your relationships.

And you don't have to wait for a friend to read the script to you, you can move through the positions in the 'privacy of your own mind' anytime you'd like!

> *"What a wonderful miracle.*
> *If only we could look through each other's eyes,*
> *for an instant."*
> ~ *Henry David Thoreau*

Meanwhile…keep lovin' your boy!

19. Reviewing Your Journey

As your journey of discovery comes to a close, I encourage you to share what you've learned with others. Share the information, and...even better, share the stories of how the journey has changed you and changed your relationship with your boy. Thank yourself for the time you've dedicated to the task of understanding yourself, your boy, and your family in a new way. Bravo!

Take a moment to do that now...

The Wheel of Your Life

Just as you did so long ago, take some time to color in the Wheel of Your Life. You may find yourself surprised! You may find that your *one wild and precious life* is now back on track and you are moving forward gleefully!   If it is not quite there yet, you know what to do…ask yourself, ***"What do I want instead?"***

DATE: _____

Fun & Recreation   Physical Environment

Money   Health

Romance   Career

Relationships   Personal
                                                    Development

A letter to your boy

Remember the letter the Mom wrote to her 21 year old son? You may want to write a letter to your son now. Include your observations of him, the changes you've made, your hopes and dreams for him.

You are his standard-bearer when he can't see through the haze; you are the champion of his cause! Write him a letter and be specific about what you admire and cherish about him.

A letter to yourself

And finally, write a letter to yourself, as if you are your best friend. Acknowledge your accomplishments and praise yourself for your striving and willingness to change!

You may want to expand on this idea and write a letter of gratitude to others who have been important in helping you raise your boy to be a man.

Letter to my son ...

Date: _____

Letter to myself ...

Date: _____

> *"Making the decision to have a child is momentous.*
> *It is to decide forever to have your heart*
> *go walking around outside your body."*
>   ~   Elizabeth Stone

Meanwhile… keep lovin' your boy!

and

Blessings on your continued journey,

Janet Allison

20. Books of Interest & Web Resources

Boys and Girls Learn Differently! Michael Gurian. Brain-based innovations to motivate and inspire everyone interested in educating kids. Jossey-Bass 2001.

Bringing the Best Out in Boys. Lucinda Neall. Communication strategies for teachers. Hawthorn Press, 2003.

Covering Home. Jack Petrash. Lessons on the art of fathering from the game of baseball. Robins Lane Press, 2000.

Easy to Love, Difficult to Discipline. Becky A. Bailey, Ph.D. The 7 basic skills for turning conflict into cooperation. Harper, 2000.

Heaven on Earth. Sharifa Oppenheimer. A handbook for parents of young children. Steiner Books, 2006

Making a Good Brain Great. Daniel G. Amen, MD. Brain-centered principles to change your life. Harmony Books, 2005.

Nurture Shock, New Thinking about Children. Po Bronson & Ashley Merryman. A revolutionary perspective on childhood, upending conventional wisdom. Twelve, 2009.

The Courage to Raise Good Men. Olga Silverstein. You don't have to sever the bond with your son to help him become a man. Penguin, 1995.

Raising Boys. Steve Biddulph. Why boys are different – and how to help them become happy and well-balanced men. Celestial Arts, 1998.

Raising Cain. Dan Kindlon. Protecting the emotional lives of boys. Ballantine, 2000.

Raising a Teenager. Jeanne Elium & Don Elium. Parents and the nurturing of a responsible teen. Celestial Arts, 1999.

Simplicity Parenting. Kim John Payne, M.Ed. Using the extraordinary power of less to raise calmer, happier, and more secure kids. Ballantine, 2009.

Strategies for Teaching Boys and Girls. Michael Gurian. An essential resource for all teachers who want to improve their practice and get the most from all students – whatever their gender. [And other titles by Michael Gurian] Jossey-Bass, 2008.

The Primal Teen. Barbara Strauch. What the new discoveries about the teenage brain tell us about our kids. Doubleday, 2003.

Understanding Waldorf Education. Jack Petrash. A compelling, clearly written picture of the key components of Waldorf education. Gryphon House, 2002.

Why Gender Matters. Leonard Sax, MD, PhD. What parents and teachers need to know about the emerging science of sex differences. Broadway Books, 2005.

Your Child's Growing Mind. Jane Healy, PhD. Brain development and learning from birth to adolescence. Broadway, 2004.

Web Resources

www.parenting-advice-from-mom.com - Supportive parenting advice, tips, and the up-dated know-how you wish you'd learned from your own Mom! Includes Boys Alive! Bring Out Their Best! resources.

www.amenclinics.com - Education and the latest advances in neuro-imaging.

www.bamgroups.com – Advocacy and mentoring.   Making better contact with boys.

www.boystomen.org - Created to guide boys 13-17 through their passage to manhood.

www.gurianinstitute.com - Professional dev. in awareness of gender intelligence.

www.guysread.com - A site designed to get boys reading. Book recommendations.

www.laughyourway.com – For teens and parents - sex, dating and relating tips.

www.nlporegon.com – Communication skills for improving your quality of life.

www.nova institute.net - Fresh insights into parent and teacher education through a deeper understanding of children.

www.steinerstorehouse.com - Dolls, dress-ups, wooden toys, games, books.

www.simplicityparenting.com - Using the extraordinary power of less to raise calmer, happier and more secure kids..

www.whywaldorfworks.org - Information on Waldorf schools and Waldorf education.

www.youandyourchildshealth.org - library of health information about raising children and creating a healthier family life

CPSIA information can be obtained at www.ICGtesting.com
Printed in the USA
BVOW04s2359140615

404077BV00003B/205/P